S0-BFI-131

Just
AROUND
The
CORNER

1999—2000 NWMS READING BOOKS

RESOURCE BOOK FOR THE LEADER
IMAGINE THE FUTURE
Edited by Beverlee Borbe

FOR THE READER

BEHIND THE SILENCE
The Story of Frank and Ann Sutherland
By Robert Sutherland and John Sutherland

BUILDING ON GOD'S FOUNDATION
50 Years of Alabaster
Edited by Tim Crutcher

JUST AROUND THE CORNER
Compassion in San Bernardino
By Robin Hyde as told to Cynthia Sherer

LOYD AND NITA MARTZ
Pioneers in Volunteer Missions
By Lela Morgan

PORTUGAL: A PLACE OF REFUGE
By Maria João Guerreiro

THROUGH HIS EYES
The Story of Youth in Mission
Edited by Ken Couchman and Jason E. Vickers

Just AROUND The CORNER

Compassion in San Bernardino

by Robin Hyde
as told to Cynthia Sherer

Nazarene Publishing House
Kansas City, Missouri

Contents

Rev. Robin K. Hyde is the pastor of Cornerstone Church of the Nazarene in San Bernardino, California. He is the executive director of Cornerstone Compassion Center. He and his wife, Sonja, have been married for 23 years and have three children—Russell, Amber, and Rachel. Rev. Hyde was ordained in 1996 and currently resides in Redlands, California.

Cynthia Ann Sherer attends Faith Community Church of the Nazarene in Yorba Linda, California, where she participates in a contemporary praise and worship band, Living Stone. She is a teacher and administrator at a small private school.

Foreword

What Do You Say to a Hungry World? was the title of Stanley Mooneyham's book and question to the church. Following a Sunday morning worship service when 12 hungry people were found waiting on the steps of the San Bernardino, California, Cornerstone Church of the Nazarene, Pastor Robin Hyde had to answer that question for himself.

His response, spiritual insight, and leadership is the heart of this story of a remarkable congregation surrounded by what seemed to be overwhelming need. In their own loaves and fishes ministry, they took the little food they had that Sunday, blessed it, and gave it away. In doing so, they began to discover in their own neighborhood both needs and resources they could not have imagined before. And they discovered a mission of compassion that has renewed and revived their congregation.

While many people are trying to sort out the deserving and the undeserving poor, Pastor Hyde and his people have concluded that Jesus "did not make such tidy distinctions. Rather, He instructed us to help the needy regardless of their circumstances."

This well-written story describing the origins and vision of the Cornerstone Compassion Center is must reading for any congregation compelled to combine the personal and social dimensions of the gospel. It is, further, an example, if not a model, of what Nazarene Compassionate Ministries is about.

—Tom Nees

Preface

When I first began to attend the Church of the Nazarene in 1990, I thought missions was limited to distant countries in Africa. In my mind, missionaries were soft-spoken preachers who spent their lives converting tribal warriors into Christians. Missions, in short, was always "over there."

Fortunately, the Lord began to change my preconceived notions by giving our church family an opportunity to serve at an inner-city mission. Following this experience, my concept of missions was broadened to include various forms of compassionate ministry both at home and abroad.

The Cornerstone Compassion Center in San Bernardino, California, is only one of many places in the United States where ordinary Christians are bringing the hope of Christ to a hurting world. A part of Cornerstone Church of the Nazarene, the compassion center emerged as a result of God's showing us that the people who most need to hear the gospel are often just around the corner.

Rev. Robin Hyde, senior pastor of Cornerstone Church of the Nazarene, tells the following story of the origin, development, and future of the center. I am thankful to God for the opportunity to pass it along to each of you.

—Cynthia A. Sherer

Acknowledgments

We wish to acknowledge the following who have made important contributions to our lives and to the writing of this book:

My wife and love of 25 years, Sonja

Our three great children—Russell, Amber, and Rachel

P. D. James, who introduced me to my Savior

My needy brothers and sisters in Christ—rich and poor

My Jesus of Nazareth, the lowly Nazarene

—Robin Hyde

Tom, Austin, and Ashley-Rose, my "Team Sherer," your patience, support, and unconditional love truly reflect what Jesus has done for our family

My loving parents, George and Virginia Page

My gallery of encouragers—the FCCN family; our editor, Jason; Don and Jennie, Dru and Vic, Mark and Becky, LoRae, Phyllis, Heather, Nancy, Kathy, Elizabeth, Gretchen, Lara, and Carrie-Anne

Our Living Stone family—Karen, Bill, and Scott—who are continuing the journey together, bringing the joy of praise and worship to FCCN

P. D. and Carolyn James, for the foundation

Robin and Sonja Hyde for the friendship

Jim and Billie Page for the freedom

My sweet Savior, Jesus, for Your life-changing power and the knowledge that *nothing* "compares to the promise I have in You"

—Cynthia Sherer

CHAPTER 1

"Pastor, Can You Help Us?"

THE CONGREGATION FINISHED SINGING THE FINAL hymn, the doors of the sanctuary were opened, and I went outside to greet the people. Little did I know that God had a new plan for the people of Cornerstone Church of the Nazarene that day. Twelve hungry people from the neighborhood, not regular churchgoers, were huddled on the front porch of the church.

"Pastor, can you help us?" came the tentative inquiry. I realized at that moment that it wasn't a mere coincidence that René Cortez, the youth pastor, had brought a 50-pound bag of beans and a 50-pound bag of rice to Bible study just a few days before. We were already discussing the need to provide food for the community, and René's contribution was timely. We didn't know how it would be used or who would need it, but as always, God had a plan.

To meet their immediate need, René, myself, and a few other men went to the fellowship hall to prepare a dozen bags of rice and beans. After we gave away the food, René turned to me and said, "Well, I guess we're in the food pantry business now!" At that moment, we could not imagine the challenges, the demands, and the miracles that God was about to lead our tiny church through during the next 18 months.

Founded in 1946 by Rev. Kenneth Jenkins, Cornerstone Church of the Nazarene (formerly known as East Church of the Nazarene) is located in San Bernardino, California. At the time of its organization, the church served residents who lived and worked in the vicinity of Norton Air Force Base. In the 1950s, the neighborhood surrounding Cornerstone was home to mostly young families living in modest two- and three-bedroom homes.

With the closing of the base in 1992, the process of decline that began in the 1970s was complete. Once a thriving middle-class area, the neighborhood became one of the poorest sections of one of the most impoverished cities in California. Houses once well maintained were no longer cared for. It was not unusual to find two or more families living in the same house. With little or no income, these marginalized individuals sometimes took refuge in abandoned trucks or camper shells, using them as makeshift houses. Alcoholism, drug addiction, mental illness, and hopelessness forced the people to rely on basic survival skills.

The 1995 U.S. Census Bureau update reported that 41 percent of San Bernardino's population was at or below the poverty level. This means that al-

A typical house in the neighborhood

most half of the city's population earned less than $6,500 a year.

When I came to the church in the fall of 1992, it didn't take a spiritual giant to see the needs of the community. The chain-link fences, locked gates, and run-down trailer parks spoke volumes about the area's socioeconomic conditions. The fact that one of my first duties as pastor involved filing an insurance claim for a recent break-in highlighted the moral and spiritual depravity of the neighborhood.

I came to Cornerstone Church after serving five years as associate pastor of the Faith Community Church of the Nazarene in Yorba Linda, California. Yorba Linda is an upscale, affluent California community. The contrast between where I had been and where I found myself was not only startling but heart-wrenching. Yet I knew that God had been preparing me throughout my life for this new assignment.

Regrettably, I was used up—literally consumed —by the drug and cultural revolution of the late 1960s and early 1970s. By the time I was 22 years old, I had been diagnosed as a chronically hopeless alcoholic and drug addict. In fact, I was so despondent that I attempted suicide on three separate occasions.

One night, in a drunken stupor, I wandered into the children's nursery of Hillcrest Church of the Nazarene in Vancouver, Washington. There I met a man whose compassion and mercy clearly demonstrated the love of Jesus Christ for me. Pastor P. D. James's acceptance of me in all of my ugliness, sin, and unworthiness afforded me the opportunity to meet the Savior of the World.

Now, 13 years later, I found myself staring into the eyes of what I had been so many years before. The despair, the pain, and the lack of trust that characterized these 12 hungry people thrust us together. Before anyone realized what was happening, God used our meager supply of beans and rice to create an open door for Cornerstone Church of the Nazarene. After that Sunday, our ministry took on a new focus.

In retrospect, it is clear God had been working in the hearts and minds of the church board. For over a year, the commission to "go into all the world and proclaim the good news" had been very heavy on their hearts (Mark 16:15, NRSV). We were actively searching for ways to bring Jesus to an area clearly in need of His love.

At that time, out of 65 church members, only two families were from the surrounding neighborhood. The rest of our attendance consisted of families living in middle-class communities such as Redlands, Yucaipa, and Loma Linda. As a result, the differences between our congregation and the local community were as striking as those of the Hebrew children and the Samaritans. Our people did not experience life as a constant struggle for survival, as did so many of our neighbors. Understanding their plight and reaching them with a servant's heart would take much prayer and commitment.

As the church board prayed for God's guidance, we realized the church needed to change. Every time we left the parking lot, we were reminded of the mission field right in front of us. Still, we did not know how to begin dealing with the situation.

Out of a deep desire to evangelize the neighborhood, some church members began walking through the community on Sunday afternoons, stopping at each house to pray for the inhabitants. At first, the people did not seem very receptive. Families with young children, the elderly, and the gang members were particularly cautious. Most people wondered why a group of white, middle-class people were walking around in their neighborhood. Gradually, however, the people in this beaten-down area came to accept and expect our presence.

Pastor Hyde and wife, Sonja, in front of the church (ready to begin prayer walking).

"Prayer walking" brought us all to an awareness of the realities of life in the neighborhood. Almost immediately, everyone involved began to sense the endless number of possibilities for ministry. God's vision for our lives together continued to take shape, and after a few weeks, the church board voted to organize and incorporate a separate compassionate ministries center.

The board designed Cornerstone Compassion Center in an effort to meet both the temporal and spiritual needs of our community. In the midst of following the Lord's direction, we had to deal with questions about the purpose of Christ's Church in the world. Soon, the board realized that the Great Commission entailed care for the needy, whether they "deserved" the blessings of the gospel or not. This awakening shook us to the very core of our being.

The temptation to decide who deserved help was a stumbling block that threatened to undermine God's purposes for our lives as well as the lives of our neighbors. In Matt. 25, Jesus tells us that His followers gain entrance to the Kingdom by feeding the hungry, giving water to the thirsty, and clothing the naked. But which hungry, which thirsty, and which naked were we supposed to help? We seemingly couldn't get past these questions.

Some of us argued that we shouldn't help people that put themselves in the situations that caused their poverty. But as we continually went back to Jesus' words and actions in Scripture, it became clear that He did not make such tidy distinctions. Rather, He instructed us to help the needy regardless of their circumstances.

For us to grow into a healthy community of faith, God had to confront us with our own preconceived ideas and prejudices. Each of us had to resist the temptation to place boundaries on God's grace. Only then could we minister effectively in the name of Jesus.

The Lord's direction for our ministry required change. Seemingly, every person on earth has some level of built-in resistance to change. Viewed positively, this mechanism serves to protect the church from making foolish and rash decisions. However, problems occur when it is an excuse for not following the Holy Spirit. Above all else, God wants His people to be open to the Spirit so that we might accomplish His will in our world.

During this time, the Holy Spirit compelled

each member of our church to evaluate his or her reasons for being a part of the congregation. This process led to a refined and strengthened ability to see where each individual fit into our overall ministry. Our new vision allowed us to see that God uses both hands-on and behind-the-scene supporters to accomplish His good work.

Having worked through these issues, some of the church members began handing out "subsistence level" groceries three days a week to people in need. This presented another challenge—we had not budgeted to fund this endeavor. At first, we attempted to meet the need by providing ramen noodles, beans, and rice purchased from our own personal finances. But then, we realized our system would stretch us to the limit within a short matter of time.

In the first month, we distributed food to 125 people. Each bag held three packages of ramen noodles, one pound of rice, one pound of beans, and a loaf of bread—not much for the average family to live on. Hopefully, it at least provided some nourishment to fill the void.

To strengthen our dwindling resources, we contacted area food banks. They, too, were finding it difficult to provide for the overwhelming needs in the area. Then, Pastor Kenn Coil of the Temecula (now Gateway) Church of the Nazarene came to our aid. He put us in touch with a Salvation Army warehouse, and they donated a surplus of bread during each of the next four months. This gave us the ability to provide assistance while continuing to seek other sources of food.

Russell Hyde *(left)* and Tim Isom *(right)* from Cornerstone accepting Inland Harvest delivery.

The desire to provide food for the community, which by this time had grown to 500 hungry people per month, drove us to our knees in prayer. In turn, God began to work behind the scenes to bring together resources from some of the most unlikely places.

In addition to my duties as pastor of Cornerstone Church of the Nazarene, I drive a shuttle bus part-time for the nearby University of Redlands. One day, while waiting at the car wash to clean one of the vans, a posted business card caught my eye: "Inland Harvest—Food Raisers, not Fund-Raisers." I contacted their organization that day.

Without my knowing it, my wife, Sonja (also an employee of the University of Redlands), had already met Barbara Wormser, director of Inland

Harvest. Was this just a coincidence? Sonja and I didn't think so. God was making the connections on our behalf. Soon Inland Harvest was providing weekly deliveries of bread, pizza, and other food items salvaged from local restaurants, hospitals, and cafeterias.

God made another connection through Sonja's work at the university. Annually, the United Methodist Church holds its regional conference on the campus. The event requires many planning meetings between Sonja and pastors and lay leaders of the United Methodist denomination. At one of these meetings, Sonja had the opportunity to share my testimony, which includes being raised in the United Methodist Church. She also talked about the ministry taking place at Cornerstone Compassion Center. After the meeting, a gentleman named Louis Fry identified himself as the pastor of St. Paul's United Methodist Church in San Bernardino and requested a meeting with me. Fortunately, we were able to get together and discuss common issues and needs.

At that time, Rev. Fry was serving as president of the San Bernardino Clergy Association. A couple of months later, he asked me to preach at the city-wide Good Friday service. Following worship, the clergy association gave Cornerstone Compassion Center the love offering collected at the service.

When the clergy association presented us with a check for the offering, I had the opportunity to meet Rabbi Hillel Cohn, the leader of the Congregation Emanu El, the Jewish synagogue in San

Rabbi Hillel Cohn

Bernardino. He asked me if we could use more food and offered to provide us with canned goods on a monthly basis.

It was amazing to witness how the Lord answered our prayers. To our delight, He motivated several diverse groups to help the needy of our forgotten section of the city.

Other resources came to the compassion center as the result of an unfortunate incident. On Christmas Day 1995, our church was broken into for the 22nd time in 24 months. We lost a keyboard, a hedge trimmer, and several other items. Suddenly the media focused its attention on Cornerstone's plight, and a local Lutheran church was moved to contact their own national compassionate services. To our surprise, they responded by making a donation to our ministry.

Also in response to the media attention, a local alarm company donated a theft prevention system that now protects the compassion center. Within the same time frame, a young Catholic man heard about our ministry and began what would become a monthly grocery delivery of 15 to 20 bags of groceries. For us, these are just some of the examples of how God turns difficult circumstances into blessings.

For some people, it was difficult to understand why the people we were trying to help would steal from us. There was a time when churches were considered "sacred ground" and thereby off-limits to criminal activity. Unfortunately, that is no longer the case.

In a sin-filled world where poverty, despair, and addiction rule the day, anything and everything has become a target. It is hard to believe that items ranging from mops and vacuums to coffeepots, computers, and food would attract the attention of criminals. But when people are hurting and living life without a moral compass, they will do anything to ease the pain.

The solution to this never-ending cycle of pain is found in the atoning blood of Christ. God is in the business of restoration, and we believe He has placed Cornerstone Compassion Center and the Church of the Nazarene on Third Street for that purpose. Through the efforts of finite people, the Lord transforms some of His lost sheep into shepherds. In these miracles, we have come to see our place in God's plan for our city. Soul by soul, God is reclaiming this neighborhood for His kingdom.

CHAPTER 2

A Lesson from God

SOMETIMES THE TEACHERS GOD SENDS INTO OUR lives are very hard to recognize. Some are brilliant. Others are funny. Some are difficult and challenge our understanding. But ultimately, through God's grace, they deliver the lesson He wants us to learn.

Roy was that kind of a teacher. He came our way when we were tearing the roof off the sanctuary. At least nine leaks and excessive water damage were causing the ceiling to fall.

One Saturday morning, while the men of the church were busily pulling off damaged shingles, Roy stopped by to see what we were doing. In the midst of all the work going on, the answer seemed quite obvious. That was my first clue that Roy was different.

Taking a closer look, I noticed he was wearing a thin T-shirt and white gym shorts that barely covered his gaunt frame on this chilly February day.

He seemed oblivious to the weather and to his surroundings.

To my surprise, Roy asked if he could help in any way. I directed him to pick up the scattered shingles and toss them into the nearby dumpster. He stayed with this task for a few minutes before asking if we had any hot chocolate and sandwiches. Without waiting for an answer, he added, "If you don't, I can make some." He told us he would come back tomorrow, and just as quickly as he had come, he disappeared.

In that brief encounter, I did not realize God was planning to use Roy to teach me and our church family that some people can be very difficult to love. In a few months, none of us would be the same. As Roy began coming back to the church, I learned about his troubled past.

Roy suffered from paranoid schizophrenia. He began to display symptoms in the early 1970s and was hospitalized for a number of years. Then, like many mentally ill patients in the 1980s, he was released to the care of a guardian. Unable to cope with the demands placed upon him by society, Roy drifted in and out of managed care facilities, boarding homes, and homelessness. However, Roy's story is not a unique one. There are thousands of "Roys" in every city throughout the United States. The mentally ill are like modern-day lepers. They are untouchables in a disposable society.

How the church responds to the plight of the mentally ill is one way to determine the degree to which it is fulfilling the commands of Jesus. Christ calls every Christian to reach out to them. Every Spirit-led church I have been a part of has exhibited a place in its heart for people with special needs.

In our efforts to help Roy, many church members had conversations with his parents. They indicated that Roy began showing signs of schizophrenia during his late teen years. Until that point in his life, Roy attended church on a regular basis. Now, although his family cared deeply for him, Roy seemed incapable of returning their love. They supported his relationship with Cornerstone Church and hoped we could help him.

Roy represented a special challenge for our church. With most of his basic needs met at a local rooming house, Roy had time on his hands. Soon he became a fixture at Cornerstone Church, continuously asking questions and interrupting conversations. Yet at the same time, he was unable to complete an idea or logical thought. His need to constantly be at the center of everyone's attention was not only tiring but very frustrating. To make matters worse, he often chose inappropriate times to tell jokes.

Roy also considered himself a ventriloquist. During worship, he would attempt to throw his voice, imitate birdcalls, and make several other disruptive noises. At Bible study, he would break out singing popular tunes or carry on conversations with himself out loud. These idiosyncrasies not only made Roy unpopular but also caused people to go out of their way to avoid him.

In our efforts to deal constructively with Roy, one of the toughest issues involved his frequent delusions. For example, when individuals in the church were speaking with one another, Roy automatically assumed they were talking about him. This caused him to react inappropriately toward others. At times, he confronted church members about his suspicions in an irrational manner.

As a church, we spent an enormous amount of time and energy redirecting Roy's thoughts and conversations. For instance, he was prone to discuss sex and alternative lifestyles without considering that his listeners were teenagers and women. Board members worked hard at channeling his discussions toward other topics and urged him to direct sensitive issues to me or to the men of the church.

In addition to making crude comments, Roy was apt to invade people's sense of personal space. While talking, he moved his feet in a repetitious pattern and thrust his face within inches of a person's nose. In response, we were constantly admonishing him to step back into his own space. Often he refused to accept our direction and moved even closer to his target audience.

Treatment for Roy's disease involved monthly injections of medication. This was supposed to relieve some of the symptoms of schizophrenia. Unfortunately, the side effects often stimulated strange and repetitive behavior.

Although it was difficult, several members of the church tried to help Roy see the picture of reality shared by almost everyone else. Before long, they realized it was going to be a never-ending process. Nevertheless, it was part of our commitment to meet his needs.

Being consistent and committed to someone that cannot respond in a similar manner requires the strength and love of Christ. In our own relationship with Christ, He is forever faithful to us, regardless of our level of devotion to Him. As people who live by grace, we are responsible to love others with the same unconditional love God has shown to us.

Feeling encroached upon and taken advantage of was an inevitable part of extending God's grace to Roy. The lessons God taught us through the experience were not easy to learn. In many ways, we are still learning them today.

Roy did not realize God was using him to teach us about life in the kingdom of God. At the time, we could not see that the issues Roy presented by simply being himself would become everyday encounters for the people of Cornerstone Church.

CHAPTER 3

Disturbing the Comfortable

FROM THE OUTSET, LANCE AND ESTHER'S attendance disturbed our congregation. Mildly
retarded, this mother and son taught us about the
type of church God wanted us to be.

The cross of Christ comforts the disturbed and
disturbs the comfortable in the same moment. With
Lance and Esther's arrival, a very unsettling real-
ization dawned on us—our church was among the
comfortable. To remain among the comfortable
meant being indifferent or casual Christians.

Sooner or later, every church must deal with
what I like to refer to as the "third-generation problem." The founders of any church begin with passion and desire fueled by the gospel message. The
second generation often gets excited by the founders' fervor, enthusiasm, and commitment, but may
fail to understand the source of their excitement.
This usually provides enough momentum to sus-
tain the church and its traditions throughout the

lifetime of the second generation. By the time the third generation takes over the church's leadership roles, they find themselves lacking not only vision but passion as well.

As a third-generation congregation, programs, methods, and institutions designed to appeal to culture and creature comfort were becoming the focus of Cornerstone's life and ministry. The original emphasis upon the gospel and its radical claims upon our lives was difficult to find. Lance and Esther forced our entire congregation to reevaluate its sense of mission and identity and to decide whether we would be first- or third-generation Christians.

Our first contact with Lance and Esther came during an evangelistic census in the neighborhood. Tim and Lori Isom, a young couple involved in the leadership of our congregation, circulated the census on Lance and Esther's street. After discussing the census questions with them, Tim and Lori invited Esther and her adult son to church.

Months later, Lance and Esther showed up for one of the church's Wednesday evening dinners. At that time, only 20 people were attending the weekly fellowship meal, and all present served themselves. Without exception, the people attending the dinner were church folk, and we followed the established social custom of using serving utensils when filling our plates. Lance's participation, however, was about to change all of that.

As a mentally challenged individual, Lance did not understand that grabbing food with his bare hands might upset others. Eager to satisfy his hunger, Lance rummaged through each dish and food item on the table. He picked up sandwiches, pulled them apart and sniffed them, and returned them to the serving tray until he found the ones he wanted.

Lance's uncustomary behavior was troubling to people concerned with health and hygiene. As a direct result of this encounter, we immediately re-assessed our method for serving meals. At the suggestion of one member, we incorporated a serving line, and church workers dished out the food. This allowed us to limit the size of portions until everyone was served. Further guidance was given to Lance on a personal basis.

Lance and Esther came to depend on the church's Wednesday evening meal. Beyond this, a whole chicken and five pounds of rice dropped off weekly by their caretaker was their sole means of sustenance, or so they thought.

Despite good intentions, our social system often turns the care and finances of mildly retarded citizens over to people who do not have their best interests in mind. Lance and Esther did not realize the government provided more for their welfare than they were receiving. Our commitment to their well-being obligated us to help secure the full amount of government assistance available to them.

Lance and Esther tried in every way to fit in with the congregation, but despite good intentions and efforts, their involvement always seemed to create conflict. For example, they tried to dress appropriately for church, but their clothes were never clean. And while Esther was fond of wearing colorful outfits, the patterns never seemed to match.

If it were simply a matter of style or appearance, there would not have been any conflict. However, Lance and Esther always wanted to shake hands and greet people with a hug. For most people, the body odor coming from the dirty clothes made contact an unpleasant experience. The odor was a strong mixture of the unwashed human body and city grime. We knew Lance and Esther needed help. Around this time, God supplied a large donation of bar soap, shampoo, and laundry detergent to the church. As a result, we were able to assist Lance and Esther with basic hygiene needs.

In addition to personal hygiene issues, one incident particularly highlighted the difference between Lance and Esther and the rest of the congregation. Every quarter, our church attended a singspiration sponsored by smaller churches in the local zone. These events provide an opportunity to get together with other Nazarenes for fellowship and food. In addition, each church contributes to the program of praise and worship to God.

Over the years, bringing snack food for all to share had become a recognized custom. That evening, almost everyone brought sandwiches.

At the end of the evening, the pastor of the sponsoring church announced that we each should take a leftover sandwich or two home with us. Esther saw this as a great opportunity to secure food for the upcoming week. Rushing over to the food table, she informed the pastor that she would take as many sandwiches as she could. Within minutes, Esther filled two huge trays with sandwiches. In fact, the sandwiches were piled so high that she had to cover the trays with two huge garbage bags.

At this point, someone pointed out that hunger was more than a moderate inconvenience for Lance and Esther. Instead, it was a very real, day-to-day concern on their part. The easily noticed differences between us and them were now being drawn in stark contrast. Most of us were the haves, and they were the have-nots.

As their problems came into sharper focus, we became even more determined to do something about the situation. Immediately following the sing-spiration, a number of individuals in the church began working on solutions to Lance and Esther's problems. However, our solutions weren't aimed at providing food and sustenance. Rather, we spent our time figuring out how to make Lance and Esther more like us.

Looking back on the experience, the church's approach to the dilemma revealed a great difference between its understanding of ministry and the manner in which Jesus related to people. For example, John writes:

> As he [Jesus] went along, he saw a man blind from birth. His disciples asked him, "Rabbi, who sinned, this man or his parents, that he was born blind?"
>
> "Neither this man nor his parents sinned," said Jesus, "but this happened so that the work of God might be displayed in his life." . . .

Having said this, he spit on the ground, made some mud with the saliva, and put it on the man's eyes. "Go," he told him, "wash in the Pool of Siloam." . . . So the man went and washed, and came home seeing *(John 9:1-3, 6-7)*.

In this case, Christ's disciples focused their attention on everything but the man's blindness. They allowed their curiosity, indifference, and prejudice to prevent them from seeing the heart of the matter. Jesus, on the other hand, did what He could to show compassion to a damaged person so that God might be glorified.

Cornerstone Church had fallen into the same trap as the disciples. Rather than meeting Lance and Esther's needs, we wanted to discuss the issues, talk about the problem, and do whatever we could to clear our consciences.

Recognizing our own shortcomings was a huge step toward developing a compassionate heart. God was clearly calling His church to throw aside its own wants in order to fulfill someone else's needs. From this point on, attending Cornerstone required all of us to forgo the comfortable church experience. Living out the vision of peace found in the gospel now meant feeding the hungry, clothing the naked, and freeing the marginalized from captivity.

Perhaps the way Christians behave at the table says more about their understanding of the church's role in the world than many of us realize. The apostle Paul certainly thought so. In fact, his first letter to the Corinthians was a response to a group of Christians regarding their bad table manners. In chapter 11, Paul shows that modeling our lives around the Lord's Supper takes practice. The world teaches people to help themselves, to eat as much as they like, and to disregard the needs of others. The Lord's Supper, on the other hand, can only be accepted as a gift. Our relationship to Lance and Esther forced us to change the way we served meals, and in the process, something else began to change as well. In more ways than we could realize at the time, God was gradually shifting the focus of Cornerstone Church toward serving others and away from helping ourselves.

A radically different viewpoint of Christian ministry began to emerge when our treasured methods and traditions were slowly and painfully stripped away. Together, we began making the transition from snatching, grabbing, and pursuing our own needs to serving, loving, and extending grace to those around us. Paul writes, "Let each of you look not to your own interests, but to the interests of others" (Phil. 2:4, NRSV). The process itself has been and continues to be painful, but it is the means by which Christ teaches all Christians to empty themselves on behalf of others (vv. 5-7, NRSV).

CHAPTER 4

Moved to Compassion

WE NOW REALIZED GOD HAD PLACED Cornerstone Church of the Nazarene in a community made up of people living with the same circumstances and problems as those faced by Roy, Lance, and Esther. The Spirit was directing the congregation to provide hope for a community in crisis.

For those living within a one-mile radius of our church, the average monthly income per family is $450. Rent and utilities swallow up this amount, leaving very little money for the bare necessities of life. It is not unheard of for people to turn off utilities to save costs. In the summertime, families often go without electricity to make the most of the longer daylight hours. Then in the winter, many people avoid a bill by turning off their water. Few people have telephones, and almost no one owns a car. Walking or riding a bicycle is the most popular mode of transportation.

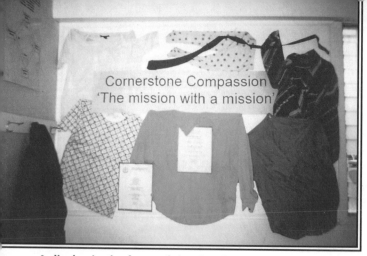

A display in the foyer of the church

Given the extreme plight of the people living around the church, we wondered if we could impact our own community for God by providing basic life needs. After all, we were a small congregation made up of people who drove to church from outlying suburban areas.

The metamorphosis from a small, traditional Church of the Nazarene to an emerging soup kitchen and mission did not occur overnight. Rather, a series of subtle changes gradually evolved into the compassionate ministry center now known as Cornerstone Compassion Center. The journey involved trial and error, introspection and discussion, and a strong vision of what God wanted to accomplish.

I have heard it said that a person can identify where a ship is headed by standing on the stern and looking at the wake where the ship has been. Similarly, moving forward in ministry required us to take a backward glance at our own tradition. Discovering the heritage of our local church, the denomination, and the broader theological tradition in which we stand was the first order of business.

A careful examination of the teachings of John Wesley and the early Methodist movement helped us better understand the fervor behind his theology. John Wesley's teachings, life, and doctrine each emphasized the importance of meeting people's social, physical, and temporal needs.

As we narrowed the scope of research, we discovered that the original founders of the Church of the Nazarene saw the church as a place where the poor should be welcomed and where entire sanctification was preached. In preparation for the 50th anniversary celebration of Cornerstone Church of the Nazarene, we searched through every available resource in an attempt to rediscover our roots. Countless hours were spent poring over newspaper accounts, documents, and the writings of Phineas F. Bresee. Bresee's vision became the heart cry of our church, and we claimed his words as our own.

The founder of the Church of the Nazarene, Bresee, comments, "It has been my long cherished desire to have a place in the heart of the city which could be made a center of Holy Fire, and where the gospel could be preached to the poor."

After this, we took time to learn about the shape of our community. The Church Growth Division at Nazarene Headquarters in Kansas City provided a detailed packet of demographic information, including age, employment status, and income census for the area. The facts were staggering and affirmed what we already suspected about our community.

Immediately we contacted all of the local assistance services to determine what resources were currently available. Then we conducted a needs assessment survey in the surrounding neighborhoods. The results of the survey demonstrated that the east side of San Bernardino, while displaying the greatest need demographically, was the least served. In the two census zones straddled by our church property, there were no food distributing services and only one Goodwill store.

At this point in time, several relationships fell into place that helped guide us toward the formation of a compassionate ministry center. Three separate people came to us in a divinely ordered fashion. We recognized God was pulling everything together in order to help our church minister to people in a holistic manner.

The first relationship came about as a result of our correspondence with Stan Ingersoll, denominational archivist at Nazarene Headquarters International. He suggested contacting Dr. Ron Benefiel, the pastor of Los Angeles First Church of the Nazarene. The church was able to supply us with information concerning the compassionate beginnings of the Church of the Nazarene.

A multicongregational fellowship, Los Angeles First is also the center of operations for a dynamic compassionate ministry center known as the P. F.

Pastor Robin passes out food to families waiting in the distribution line.

Bresee Foundation, Inc. The foundation has three departments, including an institute for the study of urban ministries; a human services division that distributes food to seniors, the homeless, and low income families; and an after-school program that offers outdoor activities and recreation for at-risk youth. A tour of this ministry center gave us plenty of information and inspiration about the possibilities for developing a compassionate ministry center.

Nazarene Compassionate Ministries, United States/Canada (NCM), was our second major resource. Tom Nees, the administrative director of NCM, U.S.A./Canada, helped direct us concerning the organization and development of a center for compassionate ministries. Through his office, the church received a start-up packet for establishing a

Third Street neighbors receiving hygiene products donated by Southern California district churches.

separate, nonprofit corporation. This information proved to be vitally important to our future, as legal separation protected the assets of Cornerstone Church of the Nazarene. Organizing the compassion center as a separate entity also allowed us to raise much-needed funds through less traditional methods.

Dr. Nees and the people at NCM also put us in contact with a multitude of compassionate-minded individuals and ministries in the Church of the Nazarene. The growing number of compassion centers reflects a widespread and conscious embracing of our own heritage and theological tradition.

One of the vital ministries I contacted was located in Hollywood, California. Children of the Shepherd serves the street people and runaways in the City of Broken Dreams. Mike and Barbara

Vasquez, directors of the center, have been ministering to the homeless, hurting, and disillusioned for several years. I had met Mike over 10 years ago during my assignment in another local Church of the Nazarene. He came to our church to tell about what God was doing in this mission area and to solicit volunteers and support for the work.

As we were forming our compassion center, I contacted Mike. He became an instant source of important information and wisdom for us. He and Barbara gave practical insight and hands-on experience that helped formulate our ministry plan. Mike also suggested I attend the upcoming Nazarene Compassionate Ministries Conference.

Thanks to Mike's strong encouragement, I went to the 1996 Nazarene Compassionate Ministries Conference held in Colorado Springs. At the conference, God used cutting-edge people in the Church of the Nazarene to teach me some of the essentials of compassionate ministry. Various approaches to the ministry were represented. Some ministers employed traditional methods in their work, while others used newer techniques. But despite their differences in approach, I discovered everyone had the same vision and desire to reach out to those who had not experienced the love of Christ.

Upon my return to San Bernardino, the Cornerstone Compassion Center board members welcomed the new information from the conference. We planned, dreamed, and prayed before presenting our vision to the church board and the congregation. The experience paved a pathway for church members to complete the process of immersing themselves in the ministry of compassionate evangelism.

To bring about the compassion center, numerous changes had to be made in the everyday life of the church. For example, as we came to terms with the church's new priorities, building and room usage had to be rearranged. The center also required a very distinct change in the church's strategy for ministry. Individual and corporate fears had to be identified, discussed, and dealt with in a productive manner.

The influx of people with many needs and vastly different social, economic, and lifestyle backgrounds was an intrusion into the normal routine established over the years. Church functions considered a vital part of the life of any congregation had to be reconfigured to accommodate our neighbors. For instance, the compassion center forced us to rethink the manner in which we prepared for potluck dinners.

Like any other group of Nazarenes, our church enjoys potlucks regularly. In fact, it is not unusual to have dinner together toward the end of every month, as potlucks are always great times of fellowship and community building. But when compassionate ministry added a large number of people who lacked the means to contribute items of food, the dynamics changed considerably. Many of the new guests were not interested in fellowship. They came only to fill their empty stomachs. Issues like this seemed to confront us every day. In many ways they still do.

The process of becoming a compassionate ministry center is both a stretching and wonderfully painful challenge. However, through all of the struggles, we now have a clearer vision of what God is doing in the community. Through the power of the Spirit, God has moved Cornerstone Church to compassion.

CHAPTER 5

Up on the Housetop

EVERY CHURCH MUST EVENTUALLY ASK THE question, "What responsibility do we have to our parish—to the local community that surrounds our physical building?" In many ways, this question became the focal point of weekly discussions. Above all, the members of the church believed God wanted us to reach out to the hurting, hopeless, and helpless in our area. Naturally, we looked forward to meeting the challenge some days more than others.

If you took a tour of the area surrounding Cornerstone Church, you would immediately notice the run-down condition of the neighborhood—urban tenements with barking dogs, discarded car parts, and signs cautioning you to Stay Away. Clusters of young men dressed in gang attire hang out on the street corners. This area is our parish.

In light of the character of our parish, Cornerstone Church constantly struggles to answer two questions. First, how do we make our presence known to the community and impact the neighborhood for Christ with very limited resources and even less formal training? Second, how can we help the people in our parish realize they are a part of our faith community?

In the two years preceding the formation of Cornerstone Compassion Center, we had heard about an intriguing ministry concept known as "prayer walking" (mentioned earlier). This unique form of ministry was introduced to us by the JESUS Film Partnership. Spearheaded by Campus Crusade for Christ, the goal was to bring a video-formatted presentation of the gospel into every household in the city of San Bernardino. And although we could not afford to purchase the video for community distribution, we used the evangelism methods recommended by the sponsors of the project.

For our congregation, prayer walking meant going into our neighborhood and bathing the homes, the businesses, and the people of the community in prayer. We petitioned God to change the hearts of the people, and we asked Him to protect, provide for, and prosper the people of the area. Finally, we prayed for God to draw our neighbors to Cornerstone Compassion Center that we might share the peace of Christ with them.

We first incorporated prayer walking during our fall evangelistic impact campaign. On the first evening, only 5 people went prayer walking. Thankfully, the number grew to 15 and then 20 on the second and third nights respectively. By the final evening, our group had grown to 30 people.

Our approach was simple. We walked together in a group praying for the neighborhood, talking to people on the street, and sharing the vision of how God could make a difference in their lives. The evenings also included the distribution of literature and prayer for specific requests.

We finished the project feeling an impact had been made—if not in the neighborhood, then at least in the hearts of Cornerstone members. God was changing us by allowing us to see firsthand what life was really like in our community. Walking up and down each street gave us a new understanding of the challenges the residents face on a daily basis.

Impressed by the impact of our prayer walks, we secured enough funds to purchase 100 *Jesus* Film videos. In the first week of the distribution process, we assigned 25 homes to each pair of walkers. In turn, they walked the streets of their assignments, praying for the inhabitants of each house. The second week, the walkers distributed a flyer to each of their assigned homes. The flyer indicated they would return in one week to give away a free video about the life of Jesus.

During the third and fourth weeks, we prayed in front of the homes, distributed the video, and followed up with those who received it. In the fifth week, we conducted a census among those who viewed the video. A number of people said they watched the video and prayed to receive Christ into their hearts. In total, 37 new Christians came into the Kingdom through the project.

Afterward, we knew there was a great need for this ministry in our neighborhood. Unfortunately, we could not afford the cost of the project on a continuing basis at that time. Yet through our experience, we realized God was facilitating a positive relationship between the center and the surrounding neighborhood. Through the process, He was breaking down the us-versus-them barriers often sensed by both sides.

We integrated prayer walking into our regular ministry the following fall. We committed to go up and down the streets of our parish two Sundays per month, praying for Christ to transform the area through the power of the Holy Spirit. We particularly prayed for God to terminate the stranglehold that drugs, alcohol, and violence had on the community.

In the beginning, this semimonthly ministry was not fully accepted by the neighborhood. Many people were suspicious of intruders and wary of secret motives. However, as we continued to be available to the people, they slowly began to respond.

Eventually, the people met us at their gates, asking us to pray for them. The use of a large walking stick by members of the prayer walking teams made us easy to identify. As we continued the ministry, the attitude toward us continued to change.

In December we added Christmas caroling to our trips. During one of these journeys, we met a man whose life God would eventually intertwine with the life of the church. His story is just one of the many fruits of Cornerstone's prayer-walking ministry.

✳   ✳   ✳

When we first met him, Tony was making repairs to the rooftop of a neighborhood home. On the spur of the moment, the leader of the carolers suggested we sing the modern Christmas song "Up on the Housetop." The entire team began to sing the tune, and it caught Tony's attention. Intrigued, he came down from the roof to find out who we were and why we were in the neighborhood singing Christmas carols.

I would like to say we presented the gospel to Tony at that precise moment. I wish I could report that he got down on his knees and prayed for God's forgiveness and accepted Christ as his Savior. Unfortunately, that wasn't the case with Tony. There were many issues in Tony's past he had not dealt with. His father had died, and Tony had broken his leg on the day of the funeral. Due to the extent of his leg injury, he was unable to work for many months.

Around this same time, Tony's wife left him. Problems remaining from his service in the Vietnam War were haunting him, and he continued to experience financial difficulty. In short, his refusal to deal with these issues constantly weighed him down. Denial caused Tony to doubt himself, and this left him devoid of any sense of purpose in life.

To further complicate matters, Tony had little religious upbringing and did not know he could rely on God during difficult times. Due to a lack of exposure to the revelation of God in Scripture, Tony was unaware that God loved him and sent His only Son to die for him. Without this strong anchor,

Tony had been wandering aimlessly through life. Nevertheless, if a person saw Tony at the grocery store or waiting at the bus stop, the fact that he was suffering would not be obvious.

Like many of the people in our area, Tony was technically homeless. Though he could usually find a place to stay, he was without a permanent address or home. From night to night, he was not sure where his head would rest. Many people in this area gladly accepted whatever shelter was available and lived in it. Whether it be an abandoned shack, a dirty garage, or an old camper shell, they found a way to convert almost anything into temporary housing. Often, they adapted to whatever provided a dry spot in wet weather or shady shelter during the blistering heat of summer.

Homelessness of this sort is not usually dealt with by social service agencies. People living in these conditions often go undiscovered by the welfare system, as they do not hold down jobs like most members of society. They simply do whatever is necessary to make it through the day. For some, begging and stealing become routine methods of survival.

Tony became interested in Cornerstone Church after our Christmas encounter. At first he hung around the church to watch what we were doing. After a while he got involved bagging rice and sorting donated food. Tony also started sweeping the floors and cleaning up the church grounds. Eventually he became one of the church's right-hand men in our efforts to facilitate God's work in our neighborhood.

In addition to working with us, Tony attended church on Sundays. Needless to say, he had many questions about the Christian faith. He wanted to know if he could trust the Bible. He was hungry for truth, and God was helping us to provide ideas and concepts in digestible chunks. Nevertheless, Tony could not believe that the story of Christ was true.

Around this time, a certain newspaper article was published that indicated the city of San Bernardino was searching for sites to serve lunches to children during the summer months. The Compassion Board contacted the city for more information, and after spending time in prayer, we offered our site for this purpose.

When the city official in charge came out to inspect our property, many of Cornerstone's members knew this project was part of God's vision for us. Upon finding out the compassion center was also a church, she asked if we could present a program for the children in addition to serving lunches. She suggested we offer a Vacation Bible School at the same time. This would encourage neighborhood children to take part in the lunch program. The definitive line between church and state was being crossed, and of course, we were happy to oblige.

The commitment made to the lunch program created some additional concerns. The program involved a daily obligation of four hours' worth of work. This included preparing the dining hall, receiving the food as it arrived, and maintaining the standards of food service required by the state. During this time, we were also operating basic grocery and clothing distribution services. Consequently, the lunch program forced us to locate additional summer workers to serve the children.

That summer, though not yet having made a commitment to Christ, Tony joined us in this new venture. He cared for the children with a servant's heart, directed them to the dining hall, helped seat them, and cleaned up the inevitable spills associated with large groups of hungry children. It was evident to everyone that Tony had a unique ability to serve children and enjoyed attending to their needs.

The interaction between Tony and the other volunteers proved to be a great time of training and discipleship. It also provided the basis for new friendships. There were many opportunities to talk about God during lunch preparations and throughout the cleanup process as well. Together, church members and workers shared their faith and discussed their experiences of God's unfailing love.

When the summer came to an end, Tony and the other workers expressed a desire to maintain the fellowship that had been created. We responded to their request by offering a Tuesday morning Bible study for both the workers and the neighborhood people. Tony faithfully attended Bible study every week; in fact, he didn't miss a single lesson.

In a short time, Tony began to see the love of God through the Scriptures. He also came to understand how this love was being demonstrated to him, the children, and the other workers. Tony knew God had been moving in his life, and he was beginning to accept God's love for him.

Tony getting baptized

Eventually Tony confessed his belief in Jesus Christ. As with everything else in his life, Tony's decision to believe and embrace Christ came about in a simple and matter-of-fact way. One day during a worship service, without drawing attention to himself, Tony accepted Christ as his Lord and Savior.

We baptized Tony later that year, an event signifying that his life now belonged to Christ. The event was a time of great celebration for everyone involved with the compassion center.

As with every Christian's spiritual life, Tony's journey has just begun. There have already been mountaintop moments and time spent in the valleys. Choosing to follow Christ has not made his life easier, nor has it provided an effortless path. Yet through it all, the Lord has remained faithful to Tony, and Tony has remained faithful to Him.

Tony shows his Christmas spirit while distributing food to his neighbors.

CHAPTER 6

A Few Laborers Are Sometimes Enough

VOLUNTEER-BASED ORGANIZATIONS CAUSE ONE TO wonder where workers will be found to accomplish what needs to be done. Securing dependable help is especially challenging during the start-up phase of an organization.

As Cornerstone Church of the Nazarene developed its emphasis on compassionate ministry, the need for volunteers was suddenly greater than at any previous time in the church's history. Having spent many years in the restaurant industry, my prior experience helped us manage the initial handling, storage, and serving of food. But once we began receiving food from such organizations as Inland Harvest, the Salvation Army, and Congregation Emanu El, we had to improve our methods. Someone had to deliver donated food to the compassion center location. Then each delivery had to

Tony *(top)*, Joy *(middle)*, and Dana *(bottom)* on the steps of Cornerstone Church of the Nazarene.

be sorted into appropriate distribution amounts before it could be given to the people who needed it.

At first the center was able to use people in the church, including myself, to handle the tasks of gathering, sorting, and separating the food. But when we began to make clothing available for distribution, it was clear we would need people to volunteer their time in this area as well.

Once again, we turned to the congregation for support. Several church ladies volunteered to handle the sorting, hanging, and checking of clothing items received from people who heard about our new ministry.

The weeks progressed into months, and the need to have a core group of people in charge be-

Clothes closet

came increasingly evident. As with many areas of
ministry, reality set in quickly as the task turned into long hours of repetitious work. There are mountaintop experiences in every ministry, but those are
usually preceded and followed by the tedium of
getting the job done. Unfortunately, ministry is not
exciting 100 percent of the time. However, the job
must be completed if we are going to meet the
needs of our world.

As the number of people continued to increase,
we prayed about which individuals should help us
maintain both the food pantry and the clothes closet. We communicated the need both to the people
of the church and to the people we were serving,
and we were pleasantly surprised at the response.
A number of people who were benefiting from our
work volunteered their time.

Joy, Dana, and Debra helped with the clothes closet. They sorted clothes, determined sizes, and organized the clothes for distribution. This may not sound like a big job, but we started out with bags of clothing and a couple of hanging clothes racks. We didn't even have a place to store the items. Yet these ladies were willing to work to make the clothing available to the people of their neighborhood.

Church members Mike and Tonya Hoover located some commercial clothes racks to hang the clothing on. We then took a small room located off the sanctuary and used it for sorting and storing clothes. Joy, Dana, and Debra were always on hand to sort and organize the items as they arrived. These ladies became the backbone of the clothes closet ministry. And when I say "backbone," I mean they literally lifted, toted, and carried goods from the drop-off point to the closet and made sure the items were ready to be distributed to the needy. Each lady worked diligently to provide quality clothing for the community.

The church board continually praised God for bringing such loyal workers into our midst. Joy had previously been in contact with the Church of the Nazarene in the nearby city of Redlands, where the church had helped her and her family get through a difficult time. Along with her husband and their four children, Joy lives a few blocks from our church. Originally they came to the church seeking food. Only later did Joy become a hardworking organizer of the clothes closet.

Dana came to Cornerstone because of her

friendship with Joy. Dana and her family live close to both the church and Joy. Together, Dana and Joy spent many hours working in the storage room. As they labored, they went about their tasks talking, laughing, and enjoying each other's company. Despite the difficulty of the job and the heat inside the stuffy storage room, the two women always had an upbeat attitude.

Debra, along with her husband and three daughters, lives in an aging duplex farther away from the church. She, too, came to us in search of food for her family. Then she was quickly attracted to the idea of preparing clothes for distribution. Debra also encouraged others in the neighborhood to join in the work of the compassion center.

Together with the people who helped store and distribute food, these ladies confirmed our convictions regarding the purpose and mission of Cornerstone Church of the Nazarene. As we watched the people from the neighborhood get involved in the work, the importance of the church's role in the lives of the needy became clearer than ever before. In both middle- and upper-class neighborhoods, people often have the luxury of taking part in youth sports, fraternal organizations, and health clubs. The lower-class status of the community surrounding Cornerstone Compassion Center prevents the development of such recreational outlets. Without a focal point or place to bring community members together, people become isolated unto themselves. Even when relationships are formed, they are usually based on what one person can obtain from someone else.

As a result of coming to work at the center, many of the people began to experience the blessings of community where there had previously been isolation. The compassionate ministry center was not limited to a place for religious and spiritual development or even food and clothing distribution. It became a center point around which the neighborhood revolved. People only vaguely acquainted with one another were now making the fellowship hall and clothing closet a place to congregate. As they collected food or clothing, they shared neighborhood information and discovered the dynamics of one another's lives. The experience brought us all to a deeper level of communication.

However, while the center was definitely making an impact upon the neighborhood, it would be naive to think everything was calm and peaceful. On the contrary, we experienced regular dosages of conflict. The refinement and the social niceties shared between individuals in a faith community were often difficult to find. Instead, the community members did not hesitate to let each other know how they felt about local issues or their circumstances in life.

In the midst of the difficulties, we were able to rely on Joy, Dana, and Debra's ability to act as mediators. In fact, helping to settle differences became part of their unofficial job descriptions. Then when the conflict was over, I usually took the opportunity to share biblical principles of discipleship and leadership with the ladies. Sometimes the point of a lesson would strike home, and the effects could be seen in their attempts to interact with others using newly discovered principles and strategies.

Despite my efforts, there have been times when the lessons were not well received. Furthermore, not all of the people we work with have success. The principles we try to instill don't always overcome the issues in a particular individual's past.

Cornerstone Compassion Center tries to model a work ethic and life principles that are transferable to the job market. When we do succeed, the workers become motivated to seek gainful employment. For example, Debra went on to obtain a job serving meals in a local restaurant. She used her experiences at the center to improve the quality of life for both herself and her family.

In the lives of other workers, a new sense of calling and purpose often emerges. This represents Dana's experience. She has demonstrated her faith by continuing to serve effectively through hands-on ministry to the community. She now oversees the food bank operation by preparing hot meals and coordinating volunteers for the compassion center.

As the demand for services and the number of people needing help increases, so does the need for laborers. Joy, Dana, and Debra blazed a trail for others in the community to follow. These ladies became ambassadors for Christ, representing what can happen when the faith community and the neighborhood people work together toward a common good.

CHAPTER 7

Victory in the Making

BECAUSE I HAVE LIVED IN A PART OF THE coun-
try where the snow is plentiful, I have
learned to eagerly anticipate the end of a long win-
ter. Even the smallest hint of an approaching spring
can be exciting. Daffodils sprouting from small
holes in snowbanks are often among the earliest
signs of new life.

In the midst of the hardships of life in the
Third Street neighborhood, a spiritual daffodil is
sprouting. Her name is China.

Along with her boyfriend, George, China came
to Cornerstone after being referred to us by a chaplain at the community hospital. China and George
lived in our parish area and experienced emotional
difficulties. Chaplain Dave Randall knew about our
ministry and encouraged them to visit us.

China and George were a pleasant-looking, mid-
dle-aged couple. Their outward appearance did not
reveal the depth of inner turmoil going on in their

lives. However, God eventually peeled away the veneer as our lives became intertwined with theirs.

George spent his tumultuous childhood in the nearby desert area of the Inland Empire (a section of southern California). While still a teenager, he received a gunshot wound. The experience caused a chain reaction in his life, and George became involved in kung fu and the Eastern arts. Soon he was very conversant with the teachings of the Tao, Buddha, and other Eastern spiritual masters.

George has an outgoing personality, and he was eager to share a good portion of his story. China, by sharp contrast, is very quiet and was hesitant to share her background with us. Slowly the reasons for China's reticence made themselves evident.

China and George arrived at Cornerstone prior to our first summer lunch program. They volunteered to become part of the group of caregivers and food servers. After getting approval from their doctors and Chaplain Randall, they were eager to participate.

All of Cornerstone's lunch program volunteers are required to attend a training program. Following this program, China and George began serving the children five days a week. The only exception to their volunteer schedule occurred on the first day of each month. As with many patients drawing disability from the state, they had to get monthly checkups in order to continue receiving benefits.

As the summer lunch program progressed, China and George were always present at 10 A.M. to receive the food. Then they helped deliver the food to the fellowship hall, sanitized the tables and food service areas, and maintained the food at the proper serving temperature until the children arrived at 11:30. Their efforts were deeply appreciated during this busy time of the day.

When a church and a compassion center work together, the church must find ways to create bridges that help people get from where they are to where God wants them to be. Sometimes God blesses us with servants who can demonstrate the love of God in a manner that fosters faith development. Lorena Applegate was that kind of servant.

Lorena was one of the senior adults at Cornerstone Church of the Nazarene. A volunteer in the lunch program, she was a blessing to the people of the neighborhood. Above all, she modeled a life of devotion to the Lord.

For Lorena, being a Christian meant not mincing words when it came to right and wrong. Yet, despite her demanding ethics, she shared the love of God with people in a caring and truly compassionate way. People saw how Lorena's relationship with Christ was carried out every day in her dealings with the children and other workers.

Beyond the everyday Christlike character of Lorena's service, she also took advantage of the opportunity to develop a friendship with China. The two ladies hit it off immediately, and a warm relationship began to prosper.

As Lorena and China's friendship progressed, they had daily conversations about spiritual issues and the peace God provides for His children. Slowly China began to trust her new friend enough to share stories from her past.

As China began to open up, we learned she was reared in the Orange County area. A child of the '60s, China went through the "flower power" movement and took part in the things that characterized that time in America's history. China abandoned her Christian background in search of the meaning offered by the peace-and-love society of the surrounding pop culture. She experimented with many different religions and even became involved with the Hare Krishna sect.

Above all, China was looking for fulfillment and happiness in life. Not surprisingly, she was unable to find it in this environment. Others took advantage of China's nonassertive personality, often pushing and shoving her around. Eventually she married and had two children, later divorcing and remarrying several times.

At some point, China began using alcohol to diffuse her feelings of insecurity. In her marriage relationships, she always seemed to be attracted to men who were authoritarian and abusive. Her desire to protect her children from physical and emotional abuse was a source of continuous pain and stress in her life.

Finally, the strain of abusive relationships began to take their toll on China's emotional stability. Gradually she withdrew into a hidden world characteristic of those who are hurting deeply.

As the difficulties continued to stack up, China's personality changed. She became compulsive, making up aliases in order to buy material goods on credit. An extreme sense of guilt coupled with emotional pressure caused China to take on the personalities of the different aliases. Eventually she ended up in the hospital.

As China was in need of help for both chemical dependency and emotional problems, Chaplain Randall referred her to the community of faith at Cornerstone Compassion Center. Fortunately, China received the basic groundwork of faith as a child. In fact, she had a rudimentary understanding of what it meant to follow Christ. She was not antagonistic toward the teachings of the church, and more importantly, she was open to the gospel. But in spite of her grasp of faith, China could not get beyond her sense of unworthiness. Because of her destructive past, she simply couldn't embrace the love of God.

China knew she needed to avoid alcohol and drugs, and she was already familiar with the 12-step program. She continued under the care of psychiatrists and diligently followed their instructions. Then, as she opened up with a couple of the workers, good things began happening to her. One by one, the doctors took her off the medications.

As we continued through the summer lunch program together, China expressed a desire to give her life to Christ. Throughout the summer months, we shared the gospel with her. Eventually, she accepted Christ as her personal Savior, and with her newfound faith, she began an incredible journey home.

Upon accepting Christ, the Lord gave China a voracious appetite for His Word. She pursued the Christian disciplines, and she completed the basic Bible studies available to her through the church.

China then undertook a one-year program of discipleship. In her yearlong journey of faith, China studied the assigned lessons and went through all of the steps involved in the program. After evaluating her life—seeing where she had been and what God had saved her from—many of the scars remaining from her past began to heal. As part of this process, China saw the need for restitution and made amends with people from her past.

Through all of this, it was obvious that God was performing a great miracle of change within her. This change not only was a matter of the heart but affected her personality as well.

As part of her new personality, China demonstrated a great love for people, particularly children. She volunteered to work with children during the Wednesday night program, and she ventured out to interact with other adults as well. China took great pains to do her best. As a result, she became a living example of what life can be like when a person turns everything over to Christ.

As China continued to study the Scriptures, she worked hard to apply them to her life. For instance, she did everything in her power to clear her conscience of previous wrongdoings. In fact, she even made arrangements to make payments to businesses with whom she had used aliases. Continuing the fellowship she experienced during the summer was also important for China. But more than anything else, she craved in-depth Bible study. Working closely with Scripture helped China follow her Savior and maintain daily contact with Him. In turn, she continued to grow as a Christian.

Due to a lack of emotional development, maturing in her relationships with others was very difficult for China. When a person uses substances and chemicals in order to cope with life's problems, emotional development is hindered. China had used various substances as a means of escape for several years, and her emotional life resembled the up-and-down motion of a roller coaster.

Today China continues to struggle with emotional stability and maturation. As churches emphasizing compassion, local Nazarene churches must stand ready to deal with people who have emotional deficiencies. Sometimes we simply need to lend a shoulder to cry on or a firm hand of fellowship. At other times the church must take on the intimate role of a guide or counselor to assist others toward maturity.

The process of maturity—especially emotional maturity—is an ongoing one. Growth does not occur overnight or just because people admit that they are immature. The process cannot be rushed, and it must be dealt with in a manner ordered by God.

Through China's growth in the Lord, she has maintained relationships with her family and renewed relationships formerly estranged. She is an active member of Cornerstone Church of the Nazarene and is an ever present help in ministry and

China *(right)* joined by Dana *(left)* as they clean up after serving a meal.

outreach. In fact, she now runs the clothes closet by herself and gives direction concerning sorting and distribution to the volunteers.

China's road to restoration is not over. She must maintain her vigilance against the many things that kept her dependent. With her eyes and her heart focused on Jesus, she continues to avoid the pitfalls that once held her captive.

I consider watching China mature in her relationship with the Lord a great privilege and blessing. Her involvement in the day-to-day operation of the center, as well as her disciplined approach to the nourishment of her soul, serves as a model of Christian growth for the people of the neighborhood. China is a living symbol of Christ's freedom.

China *(right)* with Virginia Day *(left)*

CHAPTER 8

Vision for the Future

IN SPITE OF SOME INITIAL SUCCESS, Cornerstone Compassion Center has barely begun to fulfill God's plan for the community. At the time of the writing of this book, the ministry activities we are involved in are only a prologue to the endless possibilities in our community. As Christians, we are people on the way.

At Cornerstone, we do not pretend to have all of the answers. Furthermore, we do not consider this form of ministry to be the *only* way to reach others for Christ. Rather, we view compassionate ministry as the way God has directed our local church to serve. Fortunately, we are only one small battalion fighting a spiritual battle in which the decisive blow to the enemy has already been struck.

Every church must strive to discover and then fulfill the plan God has designed for it. Sometimes this means taking leaps of faith and experimenting with new methods. At other times the process requires a renewal of old commitments to ideals held by an earlier generation of leaders. The experiments can be wildly successful. They can also be dismal failures. But whether the outcome is success or failure, God's people will always be better off for having served.

At Cornerstone Church of the Nazarene, God has given us a vision that can only be achieved through the power of the Spirit. We have neither the money nor the resources to accomplish all we envision for our community. But while we recognize our limitations, we also confess God's ability to transcend human boundaries.

In this book, I have shared the story of how God brought together the resources needed to get us started. Today He continues to move people, resources, and finances from more outside sources than we could ever imagine. Some examples of this include the University of Redlands Chapter of Habitat for Humanity, Redlands Trinity Evangelical Free Church, Redlands Community Hospital, and alumni from the University of Redlands. These groups are currently working to improve the buildings at Cornerstone.

It might be commonplace to think of one local Church of the Nazarene helping another. In actuality, though, this rarely happens. There are good reasons for hesitance in forming partnerships. For example, independence requires financial accountability within each individual church. Yet, at the same time, there are many urban areas in the United States under such economic distress that assistance is necessary to achieve success.

Christian ophthalmologists holding a clinic on a Sunday afternoon.

Because of our denomination's renewed emphasis upon compassionate ministries, established churches are once again helping to bring about God's vision in struggling areas of society. Six Nazarene churches have been in contact with us, and two of them are currently scheduled to take part in work projects. Local youth groups have participated in many workdays, helping to improve our site and feed the community. Student groups from the University of Redlands, Point Loma Nazarene University, and the Southern California College of Optometry have all volunteered their time and talents. This partnering of such wide and varied organizations is confirmation that God is working in all things to accomplish His purposes.

District Church of the Nazarene teen volunteers prepare food.

Volunteers work to paint and repair one of the Sunday School rooms.

At Cornerstone, we sense God is calling us to go beyond distributing emergency food and clothing, serving hot meals, and offering shower facilities. To make a significant and lasting difference in our community, we are attempting to become a Christian community development corporation.

Christian community development corporations facilitate economic regeneration that enables people to work their way out of poverty while remaining in their community.

As part of this larger goal, we have specific plans to start a rehabilitation halfway house. This will provide opportunities for teaching new life skills to the homeless and chronically unemployed.

In addition to a halfway house, we envision purchasing an abandoned home in the neighborhood. The center will use the home as an in-residence, nine-month rehabilitation program. The program will begin with spiritual reorientation and will include three months of intensive care and instruction in the Christian disciplines. During this time, the program will concentrate on Scripture, prayer, and meditation. In addition to spiritual reorientation, a work component will help people build healthier lifestyles and develop domestic skills.

This will be followed by three months of continued spiritual instruction and job assignments. Guests will work to improve the neighborhood in and around the compassion center. Through cleaning up the neighborhood and repairing run-down properties, community responsibility can be taught to those in the program. Along the way, Christian social responsibility will be demonstrated to other people in the neighborhood.

The final three months of the program will focus on spiritual growth and development, securing permanent employment, and locating a house in the neighborhood. In short, we intend to redevelop this neighborhood rather than sending people away to better neighborhoods.

Economic opportunity and redevelopment translates into new jobs and places of commerce. At the present time, with the exception of three fast-food restaurants, two convenience stores, and six liquor stores, a person has to walk a mile in any direction to reach a grocery store or other form of retail business.

The compassion center's board is currently organizing a Laundromat and thrift store to be operated by the people of the community. As a means of employment training, this will not only serve the neighborhood but also provide entry-level opportunities into the job market.

Why a Laundromat? There are two reasons. First, there isn't one located within a mile of the Third Street neighborhood. Second, we have already received 11 used, coin-operated washers and dryers from an apartment manager in Orange County. He offered them to the Salvation Army and Goodwill Industries in his area, but both refused the products because they were coin-operated. His gift of these appliances was an unexpected blessing that is already being incorporated into God's economic development plan for our neighborhood.

Some people ask, "Why start a thrift store?" At Cornerstone, we have been giving away used clothing to people in the neighborhood since the formation of the compassion center. The experience with the clothes closet reflects a vital need for inexpensive clothing among residents of this community. Also, selling used clothing helps to fund our ongoing ministry and economic development.

America is very wealthy in used material goods. As the saying goes, "One man's trash is another man's treasure." Thanks to other people's "trash," the center already has the resources to begin these two ministries. Other small business ventures and ideas will be grafted into the vision as God provides additional resources.

Compassionate ministry centers across the United States are utilizing the concept of economic development in an effort to change the plight of impoverished groups of people. In places like Cincinnati, San Francisco, and North Little Rock, Arkansas, to name just a few, small business ministries are developing job opportunities and skills training in an effort to revitalize struggling neighborhoods. These ideas are transferable to any neighborhood and faith community willing to risk doing ministry with a holistic view of God's kingdom.

Concern for the future of any community also requires intervention in the lives of children. Cornerstone's commitment to children in the Third Street neighborhood includes the continuation of a summer lunch program. Among other things, the program provides children with a safe environment in which to play.

Today, instead of a broken slide and swing set, the center offers tetherball courts, a complete slide and swing set, and a volleyball court. A fraternity group from the University of Redlands has committed to improve the play area as one of their community service projects.

Computers donated from a variety of sources enable us to create a computer lab for the neighborhood children. Currently the center utilizes the lab during our Wednesday night children's program, and plans are in place to begin an after-school tutoring and mentoring program. Volunteers from an area church are investigating the possibility of a long-term commitment to teach in the lab. Others from the same fellowship are procuring software and hardware upgrades from local businesses to help increase the quality of our resources.

Among both children and adults, the community has taken a strong interest in the computer lab. Many adults have inquired as to when computer classes will be made available for them.

Is it possible that God could use discarded computers to help a discarded community regain dignity? To motivate them to become active, productive citizens?

We believe God wants to restore the people of the Third Street neighborhood in every aspect of their lives. Furthermore, we believe individual lives are only redeemed through the holistic revitalization of an entire community.

Christmas Eve at Cornerstone, Wednesday, December 24, 1997.

At Cornerstone Compassion Center, our vision is to demonstrate the life-changing power of Jesus by taking it into the city—one life, one street, one neighborhood at a time. Part of the Cornerstone vision echoes the words of Rev. Robert Pierce (1848—1937), the general secretary of the First and Second General Assemblies of the Church of the Nazarene. Wherever there were four or five Nazarene churches in an area, Rev. Pierce believed they should support a mission or soup kitchen. He says,

"I make a plea . . . for the sinking and submerged tenth [the poor of the U.S.A.]. I believe this great and trying work belongs to the church."

The restoration of communities, in the name of Jesus, can be accomplished to the benefit of cities, countries, and the entire world!

Sonja Hyde talks with local children "in the hood"

CHAPTER 9

Issuing a Challenge

I HOPE THE STORY OF HOW GOD is working through Cornerstone Compassion Center informs and challenges every Christian. As a denomination and as local communities of faith, we must accept responsibility for our neighbors, whether they deserve it or not.

Recently the Church of the Nazarene designated the United States and Canada as a mission field. As such, the denomination must place a significant emphasis upon compassionate ministry in our own backyards. Regardless of neighbors' circumstances, local churches must embody the forgiveness Christ extends to all of us. They must look beyond any lingering prejudices and serve those who are normally on the wrong side of the world's boundaries.

Jesus instructs us to feed the hungry, clothe the naked, and set the downtrodden free. In Christ the dividing wall of hostility has been shattered. He opens the door for us to transcend our comfort zones and enables us to dwell beyond the normal routine of church life. The impossibility of reconciliation between the haves and the have-nots is nullified through what God has accomplished in Jesus

Christ. The church is only the church as it bears witness to the hope of resurrection for all people.

The first step toward meeting someone else's needs requires disposing of an us-versus-them mentality. Curiosity, inadequacy, and prejudice are three of the major hurdles standing in our way. The church must jump over each of these hurdles on its way to becoming an all-inclusive faith community.

Curiosity about the difficult conditions of other people's lives often causes congregations to talk about the problem, to form task forces to investigate the needs, and to discuss potential solutions. Unfortunately, curiosity can also become a hindrance to action, causing Christ's disciples to be ever seeking but never acting.

While having all of the information, facts, and statistics is important, it is just the beginning. Curiosity must never limit the church's involvement to simply knowing about a problem. After asking a question, Jesus always responded with action.

A sense of inadequacy is the second hurdle to be conquered. When members of Cornerstone felt led to feed people, we knew we did not have the financial and human resources to do so effectively. Even today we continue to struggle with a sense of inability to provide the means and resources required to meet people's needs. We look at bare cupboards and beat-up buildings and realize we cannot begin to accomplish the task set before us.

Many times other people challenge our program. Often we are asked misguided questions, such as, "Are you still doing that feeding thing?"

Unfortunately those asking do not realize that God has ordained this ministry and that we must continue on this pathway until He sees fit to change our direction.

Frequent reminders of our limitations buffet us on every side. Because this is the case for almost everyone involved in compassionate ministry, we are sure that a sense of inadequacy prevents others from even entering the battle. Churches that overcome the problem of curiosity often end up despairing over their lack of resources.

When faced with limitations of every imaginable kind, the churches must remind themselves that God always provides according to His purposes. Our responsibility is simply to step out in faith and to stretch beyond our capacities. Unless we go beyond our limitations as human beings, there will be little evidence of God's activity in our ministries.

Prov. 11:24-25 reminds us that holding on to what we have is sure to result in poverty. On the other hand, if we give beyond ourselves, we will be prospered. Focusing on our inadequacies must be replaced by an active confidence in the self-giving nature of God's grace.

Prejudice is the final obstacle to overcoming the us-versus-them mentality. In fact, prejudice is the greatest detriment to Christian social responsibility. Consequently we must examine our own preconceptions and prejudices at both the corporate and individual levels.

Prejudice crosses racial, economic, social, lifestyle, language, and intellectual boundaries.

Prejudice specializes in putting up dehumanizing barriers. Believing we know how things really are often allows us to justify ourselves and condemn "those people." Prejudice is like a dam that prevents the life-giving blood of Jesus Christ to reach those who are most thirsty. Admitting that we all have prejudices is the first and most important step toward tearing down that dam.

Once the hurdles of curiosity, inadequacy, and prejudice have been dealt with, it is much easier to determine what role compassionate ministries should play in each church. Meeting the needs of those outside the church's walls should be a focus of every church's ministry.

This does not imply that every church should create a compassion center on its property. Rather, every church should strive to meet the needs of its surrounding area as a vital part of its efforts to evangelize the lost.

While in school, I learned about the three Rs for laying a firm foundation for learning. Pioneers in the Compassion Movement have set forth their own ideas regarding the three Rs. John Perkins, a Mississippi minister to the poor and author of several books on Christian social responsibility, discusses the need for Relocation, Reconciliation, and Redistribution. Wayne Gordon, of Lawndale Community Church and the Christian Community Development Association, identifies the three Rs as Relocators, Returners, and Remainers. At Cornerstone, the three Rs refer to Redeemers, Reconcilers, and Restorers.

The term "Redeemers" is used to describe the role of Cornerstone's believers. We believe everything we do should be redemptive. We believe God is seeking to redeem not only people but resources as well. Redemption means to "cash in" people, circumstances, time, and every other resource for their true value. It means operating with the assumption that everyone and everything is intrinsically valuable in God's eyes.

Redemption involves forming and re-creating an ever-expanding community of faith. This includes everyone who has not heard about Christ's love. Most importantly, redemption requires us to focus on the Redeemer himself—Christ Jesus. With our eyes focused on Jesus, we can shake off the things that hold us back.

Getting involved in the redemption process allows us to become agents of change. We refer to agents of change as "Reconcilers."

To be a Christian implies a life lived toward reconciliation with God, others, oneself, and the world. Reconciliation is possible because Christ became sin that we might be made righteous (2 Cor. 5:21). As Scripture reminds us, "If anyone is in Christ, there is a new creation: everything old has passed away; see, everything has become new!" (v. 17, NRSV).

Reconcilers have the privilege and burden to work with downtrodden people. Ultimately they long to see all people set free. For the Christian, freedom includes spiritual, emotional, and social dimensions. A reconciler confronts any unresolved conflict in his or her own life before assisting others in the same process. In addition, the work of reconciliation eliminates the boundaries that separate people, races, and classes from one another.

Finally, the ministry of "Restorers" involves the recovery and conservation of everything that is good in a person's life. This includes innocence, peace, joy, gentleness, and creativity.

In the 23rd psalm, the community celebrates God's restoration of souls. Restorers do whatever they can to facilitate this process for others. The commitment to actively pursue restoration is summed up in this quotation:

"I am only one, but I am one. I cannot do everything, but I can do something. And what I can do, I ought to do. And what I ought to do, I want to do. And by the grace of God, I will do it" (Anonymous).

Within the context of the work God is doing among us, everyone must embrace the gospel story in new and personal ways. Some will continue to be supporters, encouragers, and providers. Others will receive calls to reach others for Christ through "urban guerrilla" missionary work. Either way, every church, every pastor, every board member, and every believer has to make a decision regarding his or her identity.

To what and to whom is a church responsible? How does each individual believer determine where and how God wants him or her to serve?

For centuries, believers have been asking themselves these questions. The fact that people are ask-

The children of Cornerstone

ing the questions today is evidence of the Holy Spirit among us.

At Cornerstone Compassion Center, the Spirit compels us to meet the needs of the marginalized in our own society. No matter where God has placed His followers—in a small town or a large city; in a prospering neighborhood or a poor one—there are people with real needs all around them. While it may not be as obvious as the situations involving Roy, Lance, or Esther, the hopelessness is still there.

God has placed people and circumstances in our paths so that Cornerstone Church of the Nazarene might demonstrate Christ's commitment and love to them. Perhaps the Lord is asking other churches to make a difference in their own commu-

View from east of Cornerstone

nities. Those who need to hear most are often just around the corner.

The words Phineas F. Bresee wrote on January 15, 1902, are still a challenge to every Christian today. He said, "Let the Church of the Nazarene be true to its commission, not to great and elegant buildings; but to feed the hungry, clothe the naked, and wipe away the tears of sorrow . . . [We are] gathering jewels for His diadem."

Robin Hyde *(left)* with neighborhood people during prayer walking.